Through The Valley

Bradley McConnachie

Published by Bradley McConnachie, 2024.

While every precaution has been taken in the preparation of this book, the publisher assumes no responsibility for errors or omissions, or for damages resulting from the use of the information contained herein.

THROUGH THE VALLEY

First edition. November 24, 2024.

Copyright © 2024 Bradley McConnachie.

ISBN: 979-8230280354

Written by Bradley McConnachie.

Also by Bradley McConnachie

Maidens of Justice
Maidens of Justice

Tiny Tales
Tiny Tales A Collection of Micro Fiction Sci-Fi Stories

Standalone
Humble Poetry for the Basic Christian
Tales of the Tartan: A Collection of Scottish Short Stories
Ankylosing Spondylitis and Mental Health
How To Make Prayer A Habbit
The Anti-Inflammatory Ankylosing Spondylitis Diet
Shorts for the Idle Mind
Mysteries Of The Forgotten Chamber
The Return of Deidre Tischler
Ankylosing Spondylitis and ADHD - Managing Duel Challanges
A Mothers Quest
Through The Valley

Through the Valley

Life often leads us into valleys—those deep, shadowed places where fear, doubt, and pain can overwhelm us. The valley is where the path feels uncertain, the way forward unclear, and the burdens of life press heavily on our shoulders. Yet, as Christians, we are reminded that we are never alone in the valley.

Psalm 23 tells us, "Even though I walk through the valley of the shadow of death, I will fear no evil, for You are with me; Your rod and Your staff, they comfort me." These words remind us that the valley is not the destination—it's a passage. It's a place we move through, not a place we stay.

God doesn't promise to keep us from the valley, but He promises to walk with us. His presence becomes our strength when we're weak, our light in the darkness, and our comfort in the pain. The rod and staff guide us, protect us, and keep us steady as we move forward, even when we can't see the next step.

The valley is where faith grows. It's where we learn to trust God, not just for deliverance, but for His nearness. It's where we discover that His grace is enough, His love is constant, and His plans are for our good, even when we don't understand.

So, if you find yourself in the valley, don't despair. Look up. The God of the mountaintop is also the God of the valley, and He will lead you through to the other side. Keep walking, keep trusting, and remember—He is with you every step of the way.

The Carpenter's Hands

You chose the rough and splintered wood,
The nails, the thorns, misunderstood.
Your hands, once soft, bore scars for me,
A humble King on Calvary.

Bread and Water

Not silver, not gold, You gave instead,
The broken body, the living bread.
A cup of water, a simple meal,
Your love revealed, Your truth made real.

Shepherd of the Least

A shepherd walks the hills and plains,
Through scorching heat and driving rains.
He leaves the flock to find the stray,
And brings it home, the humble way.

Clay in the Potter's Hand

Shape me, mould me, I am clay,
Make me new, day by day.
Not for glory, not for pride,
But for Your purpose, Lord, I'll abide.

The Sparrow's Song

A sparrow sings a melody,
Unseen, unnoticed, yet still free.
If You can love the smallest thing,
How much more love do I bring?

The Quiet Stream

I do not need a mighty flood,
A raging tide, a sea of blood.
Your quiet stream flows soft and slow,
Where peace and righteousness can grow.

The Candle's Glow

Not a blaze or burning pyre,
But a candle's gentle fire.
So let my life burn soft and true,
To point the weary soul to You.

The Least of These

A cup of kindness, a loaf of bread,
A soft-spoken prayer beside a bed.
In these small acts, Your face I see,
In serving the least, I serve Thee.

The Narrow Way

The path is steep, the road is thin,
Few will walk where few begin.
Yet humble hearts will find the way,
Where love and mercy light the day.

A Child's Prayer

Lord, teach me faith, the childlike kind,
With open heart and simple mind.
Not bound by fear or doubt's demand,
But trusting fully in Your hand.

The Yoke of Grace

Your yoke is easy, Your burden light,
You walk beside me, day and night.
No need for pride, no need for show,
In humble grace, my soul will grow.

The Silent Altar

No trumpets sound, no banners fly,
Yet here I bow beneath Your sky.
An altar made of simple stone,
Where I can call on You alone.

The Mustard Seed

Faith like a mustard seed, so small,
Yet it can grow to cover all.
Lord, plant within my heart that grain,
And tend its growth through sun and rain.

The Servant's Heart

To wash the feet, to bear the load,
To walk with You on humble roads.
No crown of gold, no worldly part,
Just let me have the servant's heart.

The Vineyard's Call

Not first, not last, but in Your time,
You called me to the fields to climb.
To work the vineyard, small or great,
To trust in You and not my fate.

The Lily's Trust

The lilies neither toil nor spin,
Yet in Your love, their life begins.
Help me, O Lord, to trust in Thee,
And live in quiet dignity.

The Fisherman's Net

Not many wise, not many grand,
You chose the simple fisherman.
Their nets now catch the souls of men,
Through humble work, Your truth extends.

The Widow's Mite

A coin so small, yet all she gave,
Her heart was humble, her faith was brave.
Teach me, O Lord, to give like this,
From love, not wealth, comes endless bliss.

The Open Door

You stand and knock, no force, no pride,
Just waiting there, arms open wide.
A humble guest, yet Heaven's King,
Come in, O Lord, and let me sing.

In the Stillness

No thunder rolled, no fire roared,
In stillness soft, I found my Lord.
No need for noise or grand display,
He speaks in whispers every day.

The Dust Beneath Your Feet

From dust I came, to dust I'll go,
Yet in Your hands, my worth will show.
Lift me, Lord, as You see fit,
For humble dust is where You sit.

The Morning Dew

The morning dew, so brief its stay,
Yet it reflects the light of day.
Lord, let my life, though fleeting be,
Reflect Your light for all to see.

The Empty Seat

The banquet calls, the chairs are set,
And yet one seat remains unmet.
Invite the poor, the castaway,
For they shall feast on that great day.

The Worn-Out Shoes

My path is trod with worn-out shoes,
Yet, Lord, for You, I cannot lose.
The road is rough, but step by step,
Your grace sustains the faith I've kept.

The Cracked Vessel

A vessel cracked, imperfect still,
Yet pours out water at Your will.
Lord, use my flaws to share Your grace,
In brokenness, I see Your face.

The Quiet Labourer

The plough turns soil, the fields are sown,
The labourer works but stays unknown.
In every humble task I do,
Lord, let me dedicate it to You.

The Midnight Watch

In midnight's hour, the world is still,
Yet, Lord, I see Your perfect will.
The stars proclaim Your endless might,
Even in silence, there is light.

A Child's Offering

Two hands hold tight a gift of clay,
Unshaped, unformed, a fragile display.
But in Your hands, it's made anew,
Lord, take my heart and shape it too.

The Fallen Leaf

A leaf descends, so soft, so slow,
Returning to the earth below.
Lord, teach me how to yield my pride,
And fall with grace to where You guide.

The Door Left Open

An open door, a simple choice,
Beyond it calls a still, small voice.
Lord, lead me through with steady feet,
Your humble path is my retreat.

The Silent Prayer

No eloquence, no words profound,
Just quiet thoughts that know no sound.
Yet every whisper reaches You,
Lord, hear my heart, and guide it true.

The Candle's Wax

As wax melts down, the flame burns bright,
Though it gives all, it shares its light.
Lord, let me pour my life the same,
To burn for You and not my name.

The Shadow's Grace

The shadow stretches long and wide,
It hides me where Your mercies abide.
In humbleness, I find my place,
Beneath the shadow of Your grace.

The Weary Ox

The oxen pull the heavy plough,
They do not ask the why or how.
Lord, teach my heart to carry on,
To trust Your will when strength is gone.

The Tattered Cloak

A cloak of rags, yet warmth it gives,
A humble life is how Christ lives.
Not wealth or riches draw me near,
But love that casts away all fear.

The Tiny Seed

A seed so small, the eye can't see,
Yet in its core, eternity.
Lord, plant within my heart Your way,
And let it grow with each new day.

The Narrow Gate

The narrow gate is hard to find,
It calls for heart and soul aligned.
Not many choose to walk that trail,
But through it, love will never fail.

The Grain of Sand

A grain of sand, the ocean's floor,
So small, unseen, yet counted for.
Lord, show me how Your love extends,
To those the world so quickly ends.

The Unseen Root

Beneath the ground, where none can see,
The roots grow deep in humility.
Lord, anchor me in quiet grace,
And let my strength come from Your place.

Pebbles on the Shore

A pebble tossed, a ripple grows,
How far it reaches, no one knows.
Let every deed, however small,
Be cast in love to touch them all.

The Cracked Vessel

A vessel sits, its clay worn thin,
Its surface marred, its cracks worn in.
It once was flawless, shining bright,
A thing of beauty, bathed in light.
But time has passed, its glory dimmed,
Its edges rough, its lustre trimmed.
It bears the scars of storms it braved,
Its strength reduced, yet it was saved.
Upon the shelf, it waits unseen,
Discarded now, where it has been.
Yet in those cracks, a light pours through,
A radiance pure, a golden hue.
The Master's hands once shaped its frame,
And even broken, it proclaims His name.
For He sees worth where others fail,
And through the brokenness, we tell the tale.
For though the vessel may seem weak,
Its purpose still remains unique.
It carries water, life divine,
Poured out in love, a holy sign.
So let the world see all my flaws,
The cracks that came from life's harsh claws.
For through these breaks, His light will shine,
A humble vessel, wholly Thine.

The Dust Beneath Your Feet

I am but dust beneath Your feet,
So small, so frail, so incomplete.
Yet You, O Lord, call me by name,
And breathe on me Your holy flame.
The earth was formed from dust and clay,
A simple work of Your display.
No gilded hands, no marble stone,
Just soil shaped by You alone.
This fragile form, so prone to break,
You mould anew for Your own sake.
Through every storm, in every trial,
You guide me through each weary mile.
I have no riches, no grand place,
Yet here I stand, wrapped in Your grace.
Let pride be still, let ego fall,
For in Your hands, I have it all.

In the Stillness

In the stillness, I find You near,
No roaring winds, no voice to hear.
No trumpet sound, no angel's song,
Yet there You've been all along.
The rush of life, the clamoured day,
It drowns the words You long to say.
But in the quiet, soft and sweet,
Your peace flows down, my soul to meet.
No need for wealth, no need for fame,
You call me gently, just my name.
You do not seek a throne adorned,
But hearts in quiet trust transformed.
So, let me sit where stillness reigns,
Apart from chaos, freed from chains.
There in the silence, I will stay,
To walk with You each humble day.

The Shepherd's Path

A shepherd walks where few will tread,
Where dangers loom, where fears are fed.
Yet through the night, His steps don't wane,
He seeks the lost, He bears the pain.
His staff may splinter, hands may bleed,
But still, He walks to meet the need.
The ninety-nine may safe abide,
But for the one, He casts aside.
Through thorny thickets, rocky ground,
He calls until the lost is found.
Not for His glory, nor for show,
But for His love, the sheep must know.
Lord, let me walk the path You trod,
With servant's heart and eyes on God.
For every life, no matter small,
Is precious to the Shepherd of all.

The Silent Altar

No mighty spires, no carved stone,
This altar stands in silence, alone.
No gold adorns its humble face,
Yet here I kneel to find Your grace.
The heavens declare Your vast domain,
Yet in this quiet, You remain.
No choir sings, no priestly prayer,
Just whispered words, and You are there.
This altar holds no sacrifice,
No lamb, no blood, no costly price.
For You have paid the debt I owe,
Through love so great, through scars You show.
Let every heart an altar be,
Where You may dwell, where You are free.
No grand display, no boasting loud,
Just humble faith beneath the cloud.

The Lily's Lesson

The lilies bloom in fields untamed,
No gardener's hand, no seed proclaimed.
Yet there they stand, in purest white,
A gentle witness to Your might.
They do not toil, they do not spin,
Yet dressed in splendour from within.
They trust the earth, they trust the skies,
Their daily bread from You arrives.
O Lord, if lilies can depend
On care that You so freely send,
Then let my heart learn to believe,
And from Your hand, my life receive.
Not wealth nor storehouse shall I claim,
But faith that whispers Jesus' name.
For if You clothe the field with grace,
How much more care will I embrace?

Poems Inspired by Proverbs 3:5-6
"*Trust in the Lord with all your heart and lean not on your own understanding; in all your ways submit to him, and he will make your paths straight.*"

The Straight Path

The road ahead, so dim, unclear,
The future wrapped in clouded fear.
Yet in Your word, I place my trust,
My plans dissolve; I know You're just.
I need not see what lies beyond,
When held within Your steadfast bond.
No map is drawn, no compass shows,
Yet every step, Your wisdom knows.
I lay my pride, my doubts aside,
In You, my Lord, I will abide.
For when I trust, the way is plain,
Your hand will guide through joy and pain.

Not My Own

The heart is frail, the mind unsure,
What seems so right cannot endure.
Yet You, O Lord, know every way,
And call me forth to trust, obey.
I'll lean not on my fleeting thought,
Nor take the path my will has sought.
For wisdom comes when pride will cease,
And in Your hands, I find my peace.
In all my ways, I'll turn to You,
Your light will shine, Your path is true.
Through valleys low or mountains steep,
Your faithfulness is mine to keep.

The Heart's Reliance

Trust in the Lord, so simple, yet deep,
A call to surrender, my heart to keep.
Not half, not part, but wholly rely,
On His wisdom alone, not my feeble try.
The world may shout, "Go your own way!"
But in His care, I choose to stay.
Not in my strength or clever schemes,
But in His word, my hope redeems.
With every turn, I yield the choice,
And listen close for His guiding voice.
He straightens my steps, makes clear the view,
For my heart, O Lord, belongs to You.

The Master's Hand

I do not know where paths will lead,
Yet trust the hand that meets my need.
No thought of mine can grasp the whole,
But faith sustains my wandering soul.
The twists of life, the bends unknown,
Are clear to Him upon the throne.
I'll lay my understanding low,
And follow where His mercies flow.
In every way, I'll seek His face,
And trust His love, His boundless grace.
For as I walk, He makes the way,
A path of light for each new day.

Surrendered Ways

The weight of choice, so hard to bear,
What road to take, what cross to wear?
Yet here I bow, my plans release,
For in Your will, I find my peace.
I'll trust in You with all my heart,
And let my understanding part.
Though shadows fall and doubts invade,
I'll rest beneath Your calming shade.
Direct my steps, remove the snare,
Your faithfulness beyond compare.
For when I trust and yield control,
Your perfect plan will make me whole.

The Yielded Life

Lean not, You say, on fleeting thought,
For wisdom pure cannot be bought.
The human mind is prone to stray,
But faith in You will light the way.
Each road I take, I'll give to You,
Each step I make, Your will pursue.
Through open doors or trials tight,
Your hand will lead, Your path is right.
I yield my life, my fears, my schemes,
To follow You beyond my dreams.
For when I trust, my ways align,
And heaven's plan becomes divine.

Poems Inspired by 2 Corinthians 3:5-6
"Not that we are competent in ourselves to claim anything for ourselves, but our competence comes from God. He has made us competent as ministers of a new covenant—not of the letter but of the Spirit; for the letter kills, but the Spirit gives life."

Not by My Strength

Not by my strength, not by my hand,
Do I fulfil what You demand.
No claim to skill, no boast of mine,
Can match the grace of love divine.
For every gift, for every part,
Flows from Your Spirit to my heart.
The letter fades, its power brief,
But Your Spirit breathes eternal relief.
You make me worthy, though I fall,
You raise me up to heed Your call.
Not by my works, but by Your grace,
I stand a servant in Your place.

Life by the Spirit

The letter stands, cold as stone,
Its words accuse, its law alone.
But You, O Lord, breathe life anew,
And in Your Spirit, I find truth.
My competence is not my own,
But from Your Spirit, seeds are sown.
No lifeless rule, no empty creed,
But living waters meet my need.
You write Your word upon my soul,
And through Your power, I am whole.
Not of the letter, harsh and grave,
But by the Spirit, I am saved.

A Vessel of Grace

What can I claim, O Lord, as mine?
No wisdom, strength, or grand design.
For every good my hands have done,
Was first begun by Your Son.
You call me forth, though I am weak,
Your Spirit speaks where words can't speak.
Not letters etched on brittle scrolls,
But fire that burns within our souls.
A covenant of life You bring,
A song of hope for hearts to sing.
Through Spirit's power, I am found,
A vessel of grace where love abounds.

The Spirit's Mark

The letter speaks, it strikes with law,
It shows my flaws, my heart in awe.
But in the Spirit, life begins,
And grace redeems my deepest sins.
Not by my competence I stand,
But through the strength of Your great hand.
You shape my life, You make me whole,
And write Your truth upon my soul.
The Spirit moves where letters fail,
And leads me on the narrow trail.
For not by works, but by Your breath,
I live, and rise beyond mere death.

Not My Own

Not mine to boast, not mine to claim,
For all I have is in Your name.
No letter binds, no law can save,
But Spirit life, from sin's dark grave.
You make me more than I could be,
Your Spirit breathes new life in me.
Where once the law condemned my ways,
Your grace has filled my fleeting days.
Equip me, Lord, for every task,
To serve in ways Your love will ask.
Not by my strength, but Yours alone,
For through Your Spirit, I am known.

Poems inspired by the themes of the ten most-read scriptures, each capturing the essence of the verse or its spiritual message.

John 3:16 – The Gift of Love

"For God so loved the world that he gave his one and only Son, that whoever believes in him shall not perish but have eternal life."

A love so vast, it spans the skies,
A gift beyond what wealth can buy.
The Son was sent, a world to save,
From sin and death, from every grave.
Believe in Him, the truth, the way,
Eternal life begins today.
No power can break the Father's plan,
Redeeming love for every man.

Jeremiah 29:11 – Plans of Hope

"For I know the plans I have for you," declares the Lord, "plans to prosper you and not to harm you, plans to give you hope and a future."

In quiet whispers, You declare,
A future filled with loving care.
Though storms may rise and trials stay,
Your guiding hand will light the way.
Plans of hope, not fleeting gain,
A harvest born from toil and pain.
I trust Your voice, Your promise true,
The future's safe, secure with You.

Psalm 23:1 – The Lord is My Shepherd

"The Lord is my shepherd, I lack nothing."
No need is mine, no fear can claim,
When led by One who knows my name.
Through pastures green, by waters still,
He calms my heart, bends every will.
Though shadows loom, and valleys cry,
I walk with Him, my Shepherd nigh.
His rod, His staff, they comfort me,
A table spread for all to see.

Romans 8:28 – All Things Work Together

"And we know that in all things God works for the good of those who love him, who have been called according to his purpose."

Each broken piece, each tear-stained night,
Is held within Your sovereign light.
The threads of pain, the strands of grace,
Are woven in their rightful place.
Though I may falter, doubt, and mourn,
Your plan was formed before I was born.
In every trial, Your good remains,
A masterpiece from joy and pain.

Philippians 4:13 – Strength in Christ

"I can do all this through him who gives me strength."

Mountains rise, and paths seem steep,
But in Your strength, I find my leap.
The world may say, "You're not enough,"
Yet You are there when life gets tough.
Through every trial, Your power flows,
A steady hand that always knows.
In Christ alone, my strength is found,
To every chain, I'm no longer bound.

Genesis 1:1 – Creation's Song

"In the beginning God created the heavens and the earth."
From nothingness, the word was said,
And light and life from darkness spread.
The heavens roared, the earth was made,
Each star and sea, each hill and glade.
Creator God, Your power displayed,
In every tree, each beam of day.
The canvas vast, Your love unfolds,
A story told in skies and souls.

Proverbs 3:5-6 – Trust in the Lord

"Trust in the Lord with all your heart and lean not on your own understanding; in all your ways submit to him, and he will make your paths straight."

Each turn, each step, each path unknown,
Is safe when held in hands alone.
No need to lean on fleeting thought,
When You reveal the way I sought.
My heart, my ways, I yield to You,
You make the crooked pathways true.
In every plan, I see Your face,
A guide secure, a boundless grace.

Isaiah 41:10 – Fear Not

"So do not fear, for I am with you; do not be dismayed, for I am your God."

When fear takes root, and hope seems gone,
Your voice reminds, "You are not alone."
Your strength upholds, Your hand sustains,
A love that breaks through doubt and pain.
No trial too great, no foe too strong,
For You have held me all along.
In every shadow, light breaks through,
For I am safe, my God, with You.

Matthew 28:19-20 – The Great Commission

"Therefore go and make disciples of all nations, baptising them in the name of the Father and of the Son and of the Holy Spirit."

A call to go, a mission clear,
To share the love that draws us near.
No border stops, no ocean wide,
Your gospel flows on every tide.
Through every heart, Your truth is told,
A kingdom rich, more precious than gold.
Empowered by Your Spirit's might,
We shine as beacons in the night.

Ephesians 2:8-9 – Grace Alone

"For it is by grace you have been saved, through faith—and this is not from yourselves, it is the gift of God—not by works, so that no one can boast."

Not by my works, not by my hand,
But by Your grace, I humbly stand.
A gift so pure, no claim of mine,
Could ever match such love divine.
Through faith, I see the debt was paid,
By Christ alone, my ransom laid.
No boast is mine, no pride can stay,
For grace has paved salvation's way.

Echoes of You

I trace the whispers of your voice,
In empty rooms, I have no choice.
Your laughter lingers in the air,
A fleeting ghost, you're everywhere.
Love once bloomed like wild, fierce fire,
Now smoulders low, a faint desire.
Though loss has carved a hollow space,
Your memory fills its sacred place.

The Weight of Absence

Your touch once anchored my restless soul,
Now absence leaves a jagged hole.
The love we shared, though torn apart,
Still beats within my fractured heart.
Each step I take feels steep, unsure,
A path of grief I must endure.
Yet in the ache, your light remains,
A balm to soothe love's aching pains.

Love's Fragile Thread

We wove a tapestry so bright,
Each thread a moment bathed in light.
But loss unravelled all we knew,
And left the strands of me and you.
Yet even in the darkest night,
The thread of love still glimmers bright.
Though loss may tear and time may fray,
Its echo never fades away.

Where Love Still Lives

I thought love died the day you left,
That time would heal this hollow theft.
But love does not obey despair,
It finds a home and lingers there.
In every star, in every breeze,
I feel your presence with such ease.
Though loss is sharp, love softens pain,
It plants a seed, and blooms remain.

Shadows of Us

We walked through fields of golden flame,
Now shadows stretch and call your name.
Your hand no longer fits in mine,
But love endures through space and time.
The loss is sharp, a jagged stone,
Yet through the ache, I'm not alone.
For in my heart, you still reside,
A part of me that never died.

The Language of Grief

Grief speaks in tongues love understands,
A language built on trembling hands.
Each tear translates the words unsaid,
Each sigh recalls the life we led.
Though loss may steal your voice from me,
Love keeps you close, a memory.
In every moment, still, you stay,
A shadow light can't chase away.

The Cost of Love

Love asked much, but loss took more,
A crashing wave on life's still shore.
Yet would I trade the joy we shared,
To live unbroken, unprepared?
No, let the tears flow like the tide,
For love was worth the pain inside.
And though you're gone, the truth remains,
Love's cost is paid in loss and gains.

Fragments of Forever

The world still turns though you are gone,
The sun still rises, night meets dawn.
But every moment feels less bright,
Without your love, my guiding light.
Yet fragments of forever stay,
In smiles you gave, in words you'd say.
Though loss has claimed what once was ours,
Love holds its place among the stars.

When Love Stays Behind

Loss came knocking, and love withdrew,
Or so it seemed, until I knew—
That love, though silent, still resides,
A steady force where loss divides.
The ache reminds of love's great worth,
The way it filled my time on earth.
Though you are gone, the love remains,
A quiet balm for all my pains.

The Garden of Love and Loss

We planted love in soil so deep,
A garden lush, a promise to keep.
But storms arrived, the roots were torn,
The blooms we cherished now forlorn.
Yet loss can't steal what love began,
Its seeds are spread by unseen hands.
Through grief, the garden grows anew,
And in its blooms, I remember you.

The Space Between

There's a space between love and loss,
Where joy and sorrow often cross.
It's where I find the trace of you,
In things we cherished, things we knew.
The scent of rain, the morning light,
The way the stars shine soft at night.
Though loss has claimed your earthly part,
Love fills the void within my heart.

Love's Unbroken Chain

Though death has severed flesh and bone,
Love's chain remains, unbroken, grown.
For every link was forged in care,
And loss can't touch what's hidden there.
Your voice still hums in memory's halls,
Your love still answers when grief calls.
And though you're gone, I hold you near,
In every smile, in every tear.

A Song Half-Sung

Our song was full, its melody clear,
A tune of joy that I still hear.
But loss has turned its vibrant tone,
Into a hum I sing alone.
Yet even now, the notes remain,
A bitter-sweet, unending refrain.
For love does not end with the song,
Its echoes carry me along.

Through the Pain

Love was sunlight on my face,
Loss, a shadow took its place.
But even shadows owe their birth,
To light that kissed the grieving earth.
Through the pain, love still shines bright,
A gentle glow, a guiding light.
It whispers soft, "You're not alone,"
Though loss may chill, love warms the bone.

A Quiet Presence

Though you're not here, I feel you still,
In every sunset, every hill.
Your love has left its quiet trace,
A gentle warmth, a sacred space.
Loss may try to cloud my view,
But love's bright presence sees me through.
Though time will fade the sharpest pain,
Love's quiet presence will remain.

Through the Storm

The wind howls fierce, the sky is dark,
But in the storm, You leave Your mark.
A hand that guides, a heart that stays,
A quiet peace amidst the blaze.
The waves may crash, the thunder roar,
Yet in Your love, I trust once more.
Through every storm, You are my light,
You calm my soul through darkest night.

The Waiting

In moments still, I wait for You,
Though time drags on, my faith holds true.
The quiet whispers, soft and clear,
A voice that says, "I'm always near."
I wait with hope, though I don't see,
The path ahead or what will be.
But in Your hands, my heart is sure,
For You alone, my soul endure.

The Silent Prayer

When words escape, and tears are near,
A silent prayer will reach Your ear.
In every sigh and every cry,
You hear my heart, You know the why.
No need for eloquence or sound,
For in my soul, Your love is found.
In every silence, You remain,
A faithful God, who feels my pain.

God's Embrace

When life is harsh and hearts are torn,
And hope feels distant, worn, and worn,
I feel Your arms, so full of grace,
Wrap gently 'round in tender embrace.
Through every trial, You are near,
You calm my fears, You dry my tear.
In every storm, in every race,
I rest in You, in Your embrace.

His Presence

When shadows fall and hearts grow faint,
When paths are steep, and faith is drained,
There's one who walks, though unseen,
He whispers love, and calms the keen.
His presence fills the deepest night,
He is the flame, the guiding light.
And in the dark, when hope has fled,
He stays beside, our daily bread.

A Seed of Hope

In moments when the soil is bare,
And all I see is dust and air,
I trust You, Lord, will plant a seed,
And from this soil, will come the reed.
Through time and trials, it will grow,
Into the hope I've yet to know.
So even in the barren land,
I trust Your hand, I understand.

The Gift of Grace

No more the weight of guilt and shame,
No longer bound by sin's dark claim.
Your grace has freed my soul to fly,
And now I live beneath Your sky.
Not by my strength, but by Your grace,
I find my way in this vast space.
And though I fall, I stand again,
For You, my Saviour, take my hand.

Faith in the Unknown

I cannot see what lies ahead,
The roads are dark, and fear has spread.
But still, I walk with faith that's strong,
For You, O Lord, have led me long.
Though I don't know the coming days,
I trust Your truth, I trust Your ways.
In You I find my strength, my song,
In faith, I journey, moving on.

In His Time

The days may drag, the nights may weep,
Yet in Your time, You'll wake the deep.
Though I may long for answers now,
I trust Your plan, I trust Your vow.
For every season, every turn,
A purpose blooms, a truth to learn.
And in Your hands, I place my rhyme,
For You will make all things in time.

The Road Less Travelled

The road is steep, the journey long,
Yet in Your strength, I still grow strong.
Though others walk the easy way,
I follow You, through night and day.
The narrow path, the rough terrain,
Are filled with grace, and not with pain.
For in the trials, I see Your face,
And find my joy, in Your embrace.

The Epic Journey of Grace

In lands of shadow, far and wide,
A man began a long, hard stride.
His heart was heavy, lost in grief,
For he had known both love and loss so brief.
The road before him wound and bent,
A path unknown, its meaning spent.
Yet in the heart, a glimmer shone,
A whisper soft, "You're not alone."
His name was given from the dawn,
But now it seemed, that name was gone.
The world had robbed him of his song,
For death had come and stolen long.
His wife, his child—both left behind,
Their voices faint, no longer kind.
He walked through night, he walked through day,
A man of sorrow, led astray.
In valleys deep, where shadows creep,
Through winds that howl, through nights so steep,
He sought for solace, sought for peace,
But all he found was grief's increase.
He lifted up his tearful eyes,
And saw the stars in midnight skies.
And in the dark, a voice so clear,
The Lord was near—"I'm always here."
Through rocky paths and desolate hills,
Through storms that raged and nights that chilled,
He clung to hope, though lost he seemed,
For in his heart, a faith still gleamed.
The years went by, the pain did grow,
Yet in the valley, love did glow.

THROUGH THE VALLEY

For though he wept and trembled long,
The Lord was with him—ever strong.
One evening as the sun did set,
He found a place, his soul to rest.
Beneath the stars, so pure, so bright,
He knelt and prayed, and saw the light.
"Lord," he cried, "I've lost my way,
The road is dark, the skies are grey.
Yet through the storm, I feel You near,
I know that You will dry my tear."
A whisper came, like winds so sweet,
The Lord's own voice beneath his feet.
"My child," He said, "I've walked with you,
In every storm, in every dew.
You may not see, you may not know,
But trust in Me, and you will grow.
For every tear and every sigh,
I count them all, they touch the sky."
The man then rose, his heart now light,
The pain that once had plagued his sight,
Was now replaced with peace so deep,
The Lord had promised, He would keep.
With faith renewed, he rose once more,
To walk the road that lay before.
No longer lost, no longer blind,
For in his soul, the Lord would find.
He journeyed on, through life's cruel maze,
Yet now he walked with lifted gaze.
For every tear and every night,
Had led him closer to the light.
And though the road was long and wide,
He felt the Saviour by his side.

Through every storm, through every fear,
He knew the Lord would always be near.
For grace had come, and grace had stayed,
And in that grace, he was unafraid.
The valley's depths, the mountain's height,
Were now but steps in God's own sight.
And at the end, when days were done,
The man did find the holy one.
For through the pain, through loss, through strife,
He found the love that gave him life.

The Journey of Elias: A Christian Epic
The Rise and Fall

Elias walked through a city of dust,
Where the heat rose in waves from cracked streets,
And towers of stone reached for a sky
That had long forgotten the touch of rain.
He was once a man of great stature,
A man whose hands had shaped buildings
And whose mind had spun dreams of empires.
He sought power, wealth, and fame—
The world told him this was the way to live,
And he believed.
The world gave him gold.
It gave him lands and titles,
A palace adorned in silk and marble.
But none of it filled the hunger in his chest,
A hunger that grew,
That whispered,
"More. Always more."
And so Elias reached for the heavens,
Filling his hands with everything he could take,
Believing the world could be tamed by his will.
But the riches turned to ash,
The love he thought he had was fleeting,
And the laughter of his halls grew silent.
One by one, those he cherished fell away,
The sickness came,
The bitterness,
And in the stillness of the night,
Elias felt his own soul begin to wither.

The Reckoning

He walked the streets in mourning,
Not knowing what was lost,
Not knowing how to find the pieces
Of a life that had once made sense.
He thought he could climb to the stars,
But the stars had never reached for him.
He thought he could stand tall,
But in the end, the earth was only dust.
Elias tried to call out,
To the gods he had worshipped,
But they were silent.
The idols crumbled,
The gold turned green with corrosion,
And Elias stood alone,
Watching as everything he built fell to ruin.
A whisper reached him on the wind,
A voice as ancient as time itself.
"You were never meant to build your own kingdom.
You were never meant to walk alone."
It was the voice of a Father,
One who had watched and waited,
One who had seen Elias' struggle,
His pride,
His pain.
And the voice spoke softly,
"Come. I will show you another way."

The Path of Grace

Elias turned away from the wreckage.
He wandered far,
To places untouched by men,
Through deserts of barren stone,

THROUGH THE VALLEY

Across rivers of shadowed waters,
No longer seeking to master the world,
But to understand it.
To understand his own heart.
Each step he took was heavy,
A burden of grief and shame,
But as he walked,
The world began to speak.
He saw the beauty of the earth,
Not in stone or gold,
But in the quiet ways of life.
The way a tree stands tall through storms,
How the sun rises even after the darkest night,
And how love blooms in places where no one looks.
He did not find answers right away,
For answers were not what he needed.
It was the silence,
The space,
The emptiness,
That made room for something new.

The Encounter

And then, on a hill in the distance,
He saw a man—a figure standing by a fire,
His face weathered, yet kind.
Elias approached, unsure,
Not knowing what he was seeking.
The man looked up at him,
As if he had been waiting all this time.
"Who are you?" Elias asked,
The words feeling strange on his tongue.
The man smiled gently,
"Come sit with me.

I know your heart."
For the first time in a long time,
Elias sat.
He sat without the weight of titles,
Without the need to prove himself,
Without the fear of failure.
He sat, and the man spoke.
"I was the one you sought,
In your wealth, in your grief,
I was always here.
You walked through fire,
And still you were never burned,
For I was with you in the flame."

Redemption

Elias stayed by the fire,
Learning how to listen,
How to rest.
The man spoke of love—
Not love as possession,
Not love as control,
But love as giving,
As surrender,
As trust.
And Elias wept,
For in those tears,
He understood.
The road ahead would still be long,
And the burdens would not vanish,
But he had found something that no wealth could buy,
No empire could provide.
He had found grace,
And grace was enough.

THROUGH THE VALLEY

*With the dawn came the light,
And Elias, no longer bound by his pride,
No longer chained to his former self,
Rose up,
Not as a king,
But as a servant.
Not to conquer,
But to serve.
He walked on,
Not seeking riches or glory,
But seeking peace,
And with each step,
He felt the weight of the world lift,
As he walked not in pride,
But in grace.*

Epilogue: The Path of Grace

*The journey of Elias is not done.
It is never done.
For the road is long,
And there is always more to learn.
But now he walks with a new heart,
A heart that knows what it is to give,
To love,
And to be loved.
And in that love,
He will find his way home.*

A Journey of Redemption The Chains of Bondage

Azriel was born in the dust of Egypt,
Where the sun never softened the earth,
Where every breath came heavy with the scent of sweat and stone.
His hands were small but strong,
And his back learned the weight of labour early.
He was not born with a name;
In the eyes of his masters,
He was a tool, a thing to be used.
His mother told him of the stars,
Of a land beyond the Nile where men were free.
But Azriel never saw that land;
He only saw the endless fields,
The cracks in the whip,
The unrelenting cycle of toil.
His world was the same day after day,
The sun a merciless overseer,
And Pharaohs laws the chains that bound his body.
But within him,
A seed of longing stirred.
A whisper he could not name,
A yearning for something more than survival.

The Call of Freedom

The winds changed one fateful night.
A man appeared—Moses,
With the fire of God in his eyes.
He spoke of deliverance,
Of a God who had not forgotten the cries of His people.
Azriel heard those words like thunder in his chest.
Freedom.
Could it be real?
The days grew long as the plagues fell,

And each plague a reminder of their suffering,
Each moment of darkness a call to rise.
The sky burned with fire,
The river ran red,
And in each crack in the earth,
Azriel felt the rumblings of something greater.

The Exodus

When Pharaohs heart was broken,
The people moved in the night,
Led by Moses,
By the hand of God.
Azriel walked in the midst of them,
Not knowing what lay ahead,
Only that it was something he had never known—freedom.
They crossed the Red Sea,
The waters parting as though the earth itself knew the power of their escape.
Azriel's feet touched the dry ground,
And for the first time,
The weight of the world seemed to lift.
But it was not only the weight of Egypt's chains that fell away—
It was the weight of his soul,
The fear,
The shame,
The feeling that he had never belonged.

The Wilderness of Doubt

But the wilderness was not a land of peace.
The dry winds burned their skin, and
The nights were cold with the memory of what they had lost.
Azriel walked with them,
But the promise seemed far off,
Like a mirage,

Flickering in the distance.
The people grumbled.
They longed for the flesh pots of Egypt,
For the comforts of their old life,
The life they had known—
Even if it was one of chains.
And Azriel, too, felt the pangs of doubt.
What was freedom if it brought only hunger?
What was faith if it did not bring peace?
His heart trembled at the thought of returning to Egypt,
To the life he had been born into,
The life where he had always known his place.
But in the silence of the night,
When the stars shone bright above him,
Azriel heard a voice,
Soft and clear,
The voice of the Lord.
"I have called you by name.
You are mine.
Do not fear.
The land I have promised is not far.
I will bring you home."

Shaping of a New Heart

Days turned into years.
The wilderness became their school,
A place where faith was tested,
Where the heart of Azriel was refined.
It was in the stillness of the desert that he learned the true meaning of freedom—
It was not in the absence of chains,
But in the presence of God.
He saw the manna fall from the sky,

And he ate, not just the bread,
But the grace that sustained him.
He drank from the rock,
Not only the water,
But the mercy that poured forth.
Each step became an act of trust,
Each breath a prayer.
He learned that freedom was not the end,
But the beginning of a deeper journey,
A journey to know the heart of the One who had set him free.
The chains of Egypt had fallen away,
But the chains within him were still being undone.

The Promised Land
At last, they reached the borders of the Promised Land,
A land flowing with milk and honey,
A place where Azriel could finally lay down his burdens.
But as he stood at the threshold,
He knew that the journey was not yet complete.
He had crossed the waters,
And now, he had to cross his own heart.
The man who had once been a slave—
The man who had been bound by fear and doubt—
Was now a man who could stand in the light of God.
Azriel did not look to the land with greedy eyes,
But with eyes of gratitude,
For he knew that the true gift was not the land,
But the promise of His presence.
And so, he entered in,
Not as a servant,
But as a son of the covenant.

The Legacy of the Freed
Azriel lived to see his children grow in the land of promise.

He told them of Egypt,
Of the days of toil and tears.
He told them of the wilderness,
Of the moments when faith seemed lost.
But he also told them of the faithfulness of God,
Of the One who had brought him out,
And the One who would never let him go.
He died in peace,
Not because he had crossed the Jordan,
But because he had crossed his heart,
And had found freedom not in the land,
But in the love of God.

Epilogue: A Freedom Beyond the Earth

Azriel's story became a song,
A story that would be passed down,
From one generation to the next,
A tale of bondage and freedom,
Of doubt and trust,
Of fear and hope.
And though his body turned to dust,
His soul stood in the presence of the One
Who had freed him from both Egypt and himself.
For true freedom comes not in the flesh,
But in the heart,
In the surrender to the love of the Lord.

The Last Steps

There was no final cry, no sudden burst of understanding.
Only the quiet settling of a life
That had learned to endure,
To walk with a weight it could not shed.
The years pressed on him,
But not with a cruel hand.
They were familiar,
Like a well-worn cloak,
And now he felt its seams loosening.
He sat still,
As the room around him faded
Into something less real.
The faces of those who had stood with him
In the darkest hours,
Had softened into memories,
Fading like the line between night and dawn.
There was no panic,
No yearning for a world he could not keep.
Not any more.
Not after the seasons had worn him down
And shown him the simplicity of what remained.
He did not search for answers
In the voices of the past.
Nor did he need the comforts
Of well-meaning prayers.
His hands, roughened by years of labour,
Had once held hope in a different form.
A form that promised a future built on the visible,
The tangible,
The things that could be touched and measured.
But time had taken those things,

One by one,
Until only the unseen remained,
Not to be grasped,
But accepted.
And so now, as the stillness deepened,
He did not call for anything more.
There was no need for a grand statement,
For a final testament to the life he had lived.
The truth had already been laid bare
In the quiet rhythm of daily choices,
In the gentle acknowledgement of moments lost
And found again.
He could feel the weight of those choices,
Not as a burden,
But as a thread woven through all that was left.
And though death stood before him,
Its shape vague and unformed,
He did not shrink from it.
It was not a doorway to fear,
But a room he had visited many times before
In dreams, in prayer, in surrender.
The final breath would come,
As all breaths do,
Not with a warning,
But simply as the next one in line.
It was not the end of something,
But the opening of what could not be seen.
He had long since abandoned
The hope of understanding it all.
There was peace in that,
In knowing that the great distance
Between man and God

THROUGH THE VALLEY

Was bridged not by knowledge,
But by trust.
He remembered the words he had heard long ago
Not from a pulpit or from a book,
But from the unspoken language
Of lives that had been lived in quiet surrender.
The peace that passes understanding,
The stillness that holds everything
Without explanation.
And in the final hour,
There was no need for a definitive answer.
There was only the certainty
That what was to come
Was not something to face alone.
The weight of life, of decisions made and unmade,
Would fall away like dust on the wind.
What remained was the steadying hand of the One
Who had not promised an easy road,
But had walked beside him nonetheless.

Also by Bradley McConnachie

Maidens of Justice
Maidens of Justice

Tiny Tales
Tiny Tales A Collection of Micro Fiction Sci-Fi Stories

Standalone
Humble Poetry for the Basic Christian
Tales of the Tartan: A Collection of Scottish Short Stories
Ankylosing Spondylitis and Mental Health
How To Make Prayer A Habbit
The Anti-Inflammatory Ankylosing Spondylitis Diet
Shorts for the Idle Mind
Mysteries Of The Forgotten Chamber
The Return of Deidre Tischler
Ankylosing Spondylitis and ADHD - Managing Duel Challanges
A Mothers Quest
Through The Valley

Milton Keynes UK
Ingram Content Group UK Ltd.
UKHW021059031224
452078UK00010B/688